LIVEWIRE
REAL LIVES

Queen Victoria

Iris Howden

Published in association with The Basic Skills Agency

Hodder & Stoughton

A MEMBER OF THE HODDER HEADLINE GROUP

Acknowledgements

Cover: Detail of painting by Sir Edwin Landseer, 'Queen Victoria, 1839', The Royal Collection © Her Majesty the Queen.

Photos: pp. vi, 5, 11, 14, 21 Hulton Getty; pp. 7, 18, 21 Mary Evans Picture Library

Orders: please contact Bookpoint Ltd, 39 Milton Park, Abingdon, Oxon OX14 4TD. Telephone: (44) 01235 400414, Fax: (44) 01235 400454. Lines are open from 9.00–6.00, Monday to Saturday, with a 24 hour message answering service. Email address: orders@bookpoint.co.uk

British Library Cataloguing in Publication Data
A catalogue record for this title is available from The British Library

ISBN 0 340 74726 9

First published 1999
Impression number   10 9 8 7 6 5 4 3 2
Year   2004 2003 2002 2001 2000

Typeset by Fakenham Photosetting Ltd, Fakenham, Norfolk.
Printed in Great Britain for Hodder & Stoughton Educational, a division of Hodder Headline Plc, 338 Euston Road, London NW1 3BH by Redwood Books, Trowbridge, Wiltshire.

Contents

Timeline of the life of Queen Victoria

1819	24 May	Princess Alexandrina Victoria born at Kensington Palace
	26 August	Prince Albert born in Saxe-Coburg Gotha
1820	23 January	Victoria's father Duke of Kent dies
1831	April	Victoria's Uncle Leopold becomes King of the Belgians
1836	May	Albert visits England and meets Victoria
1837	20 June	Victoria becomes Queen
1838	28 June	Victoria crowned in Westminster Abbey
1839	October	Albert visits England. Queen Victoria proposes to him
1840	10 February	Victoria and Albert's wedding
	21 November	Princess Victoria (Vicky) born
1841	9 November	Prince of Wales (Bertie) born
1843	25 April	Princess Alice born

1844	6 August	Prince Alfred born
1845	23 June	Work starts on the new Osborne House
1846	25 May	Princess Helena born
1848	18 March	Princess Louise born
	August	Victoria and Albert buy the Balmoral estate
1849	1 May	Prince Arthur born
1851	1 May	Great Exhibition opens in Hyde Park
1853	7 April	Prince Leopold born
1854	28 March	Britain declares war on Russia. The Crimean War begins
1855	7 September	The new house at Balmoral is ready. The family go to stay
1856	April	Peace with Russia. Victoria awards the Victoria Cross (VC)
1857	14 April	Princess Beatrice (Victoria's last child) is born
1861	14 December	Albert dies
1887		Victoria's Golden Jubilee
1897		Her Diamond Jubilee
1901	22 January	Victoria dies aged 81

The coronation of Queen Victoria.

1 Born to be Queen

On the morning of 24 May 1837
a young girl was woken up very early.
Her uncle, King William, had died in the night.
His ministers came to tell her she was Queen.
She was 18 years old.
Her name was Victoria.

Victoria's father was one of four brothers.
They were the sons of George the third.
Victoria's father was the Duke of Kent.
He died when Victoria was a baby.
His brothers had no children.
That meant Victoria was heir to the throne.

Queen Victoria's mother was German.
She brought Victoria and her sister up very simply.
They slept in her room at night.
They did not meet other children.
A teacher gave them lessons at home.
Victoria did not really get on with her mother.
Once she was Queen
she took charge of her own life.

From the start Victoria liked being Queen.
She was helped by the Prime Minister,
Lord Melbourne.
Lord Melbourne was quite old at the time.
He was like a father to the young Queen.
She grew very fond of him.
Victoria was popular with the people.
They were full of praise for the way
she carried out her state duties.

She was crowned in Westminster Abbey in June 1838.
The streets of London were packed.
Thousands of people had camped out all night
to get a good view of her coach.
It was at the head of a long procession.
Her Coronation went on for hours.
As she took the oath,
all the MPs and Dukes shouted out,
'God Save Queen Victoria'.
Victoria was glad Lord Melbourne was close by.

The Queen was not always so happy
with her Prime Ministers.
With each change of government she had a new one.
The next was Sir Robert Peel.
He was the leader of the Tory Party.
Victoria did not like him as much.

2 Prince Albert

In 1839 Prince Albert came to stay.
He was a German Prince from Saxe-Coburg.
Victoria's Uncle Leopold hoped that
Albert and Victoria would get married.

The couple had met two years before, in 1836.
Prince Albert was a very handsome young man.
Victoria had liked him a lot on his first visit.
This time she fell head over heels in love.
She and Albert were both only 20.

Victoria had to propose to Albert.
He was only the Prince of a small state.
She was Queen of England.

The wedding took place on the 10 February 1840.
Victoria was dressed all in white.
She had twelve bridesmaids.

Albert had quite a hard time at first.
He was given lessons in English and English law.
People at the court laughed at his clothes.
They made fun of the way he spoke.
The Queen did not talk to him about affairs of state.

Victoria had a temper.
She liked getting her own way.

Albert needed more to do.
He was shocked by the poor state of the drains
and the dirty kitchens
at Buckingham Palace and Windsor Castle.
So he made changes.
He tried to make them more modern.

The Prince was keen on science.
He liked to know about
the new inventions coming in.
He asked the Queen to invite men of science
and writers to the Palace.
As time went on people got used to him.
They came to respect the Queen's husband.
He was by then
the father of the heir to the throne.

The wedding of Queen Victoria and Prince Albert.

3 Family Life

The young couple had a happy home life.
Four children were born within five years.
The first was a girl, named after Victoria.
She was called Vicky for short.
The second, a boy, was the heir to the throne.
His name was Edward,
but they always called him Bertie.
Victoria and Albert had nine children in all;
four boys and five girls.

Their children were brought up simply
like Queen Victoria.
They had plain food and plenty of fresh air.
Queen Victoria always left windows wide open.
The children all grew up healthy
in an age when many children died.
The only one who was ill was Prince Leopold.
He was born with the 'bleeding' disease,
haemophilia.

Albert was very fond of his daughters.
He tended to spoil them.
But he was very strict with his sons.
Bertie grew up to cause them a lot of trouble.
He did not like doing his lessons.

Victoria and Albert with six of their children.

This made his father very angry.
His parents pushed him to do well
because he was heir to the throne.

Christmas was spent at Windsor Castle.
Prince Albert brought in the German idea
of having a Christmas tree.

The royal couple looked for
places to spend their holidays.
They wanted to have more time
alone with their children.

They found the perfect spot.
It was on the Isle of Wight at Osborne.
The old house there was knocked down.
Albert designed a new one for them.
At Osborne the children had a Swiss cottage
to play in.
They had garden plots to dig.
They all learned to swim in the sea.
Later, they found a holiday home in Scotland.
They bought an estate at Balmoral.
They built a grand new house.
Balmoral is still used for summer holidays
by the royal family today.

4 The Great Exhibition

In the summer of 1851 a Great Exhibition was held.
This was Prince Albert's idea.
It was to be a showcase for all the goods
then being made in the factories of Britain.
It took two years to plan the Exhibition.

A competition was held
for a design to house it.
The competition was won by Joseph Paxton.
He was Head Gardener at Chatsworth House.
His design was for a huge glass house.
It was big enough
to cover the trees in Hyde Park.
It was to be called the Crystal Palace.
They solved the problem
of sparrows in the trees
making a mess inside it.
They used sparrowhawks to catch them!

The Queen came to open the Exhibition on 1 May.
She said the Crystal Palace was
'one of the wonders of the world'.
Inside were goods from all over Britain.

There was fine china from Staffordshire.
There were statues made of marble.
Many of these seem very fussy to us.
But they showed the great skill the Victorians had.
On show too were goods
from the new ironworks in the Midlands.
There were beds, fireplaces and stoves.
Rail travel had just come in.
So steam engines took pride of place.
The Queen and her husband were among
the first people to travel by train.

The Exhibition was a great success.
On the first day, 300,000 people paid to see it.
In the five months it was on, half a million came.
After it was over the Crystal Palace was taken down.
It was moved to South London
to be used for concerts and plays.
Later, in 1936, it burnt down in a fire.

The Crystal Palace.

5 Trouble at Home and Abroad

After the Exhibition,
Albert felt worn out and stressed.
He was not strong and he often felt tired.
He would even fall asleep at the dinner table.
Queen Victoria began to worry about his health.

In 1854 France went to war with Russia.
England joined in and the Crimean War began.
Some battles were won but many men were killed.
The troops also died of a disease called cholera.

It was in this war that nursing first began.
Florence Nightingale took out a band of nurses.
They nursed the sick and dying men.
The Queen was very upset by news of the war.
She had a medal made for war heroes.
It was called the VC or Victoria Cross.

Bad news came in from India too.
Indian troops killed many British soldiers
and some women and children too.
All these things added to Albert's stress.

There was trouble of another kind at home.
Bertie, now a young man, was always in trouble.
The British papers were full of gossip about him.
Albert tried to hide it from the Queen.

Soon after this Bertie joined the army.
He went on a course to Ireland.
It was not long before he got into trouble there.
He had an affair with a young actress, Nellie Clifden.

Then Victoria and Albert went
to visit their daughter Vicky.
They wanted to see their first grandchild, Willy.
They called on Uncle Leopold and his wife,
the King and Queen of Belgium.
Albert took Victoria to his old home at Coburg.
She saw the castle where he was brought up.

While they were away, Albert had an accident.
He fell from his carriage and hurt his leg.
Soon after they got home, he caught a chill.
Albert took to his bed.
The doctor was sent for.

Queen Victoria nursed him and read to him.
Princess Alice played the piano for her father.
It was no good.
Albert got worse.

The death of Prince Albert.

He had typhoid.
On 14 December 1861, Albert died.
He was only 42 years old.

The Queen was heartbroken.
She and Albert had been married
for over 20 years.
He was the one love of her life.
Victoria was quite sure
she would soon follow her husband to the grave.
In fact she was to live for nearly 40 more years.

6 Life After Albert

Queen Victoria was in a low state for months.
She blamed Bertie for Albert's death.
She thought that worry over their son had caused it.
Bertie swore to stand by his mother
but they were never close.
Queen Victoria turned to her daughter Alice.
She did her best to comfort her mother.

Albert's room was left just as it was when he died.
His clothes and his dressing gown were laid out.
Hot water for washing was brought in every day.
Even the glass he drank from was left by his bed.
The Queen had dozens of pictures,
statues and plaques made in Albert's memory.
She dressed in black for the rest of her life.

The Queen's grief went on for months.
She kept away from people.
Her ministers still came to talk
about affairs of state.
Victoria sat in the next room
so she could hear them but not be seen.
It was three years before she went out in public.

7 John Brown

The Queen's doctors were very worried about her.
They did not know what to do.
At last one of them had an idea.
He sent to Scotland for John Brown.
John Brown was the Queen's highland servant.
He helped the Queen when she went riding there.
The doctor thought it would be good for Victoria
to get some fresh air and exercise.
So John Brown came down to Osborne.

He was a tall, good-looking man.
He had red gold hair and a beard.
John Brown always wore highland dress:
a kilt with a dark jacket and cap.
He always spoke his mind.
At Osborne, people were shocked
by the way he spoke to the Queen.
He called her 'woman' instead of 'ma'am'.

Victoria missed having Albert to advise her.
John Brown took his place in a way.
Soon he was her most trusted servant.
He passed on her orders –
even to her children.

JOHN BROWN EXERCISING THE QUEEN

A cartoon of the Queen with John Brown.

This did not go down well with the family.
Bertie, the Prince of Wales, hated him.
He did not like a servant having such power.

Even her ministers thought the Queen
was making a fool of herself.
The newspapers were full of gossip.
Cartoons began to appear about the pair.
Some of them called the Queen 'Mrs Brown'.
A lot of people thought the Queen
must have married John Brown in secret.
At Balmoral they spent a lot of time alone.
They would go out for picnics or drives.

There was never any proof that they had an affair.
The Queen called John Brown her 'dearest friend'.
She wrote many letters to him.
She wrote a book about their holidays in Scotland.
Her ministers stopped her from having this printed.
After her death the family burnt all these papers.

8 Disraeli

The Queen had another friend at that time.
This was the Prime Minister, Mr Disraeli.
He was the leader of the Tory Party.
The Queen had not liked Mr Gladstone,
the leader of the Liberals.
She said he treated her like a public meeting.

Disraeli was a very witty man.
He knew how to amuse the Queen.
He told her all the latest gossip.
Victoria looked forward to their meetings.
Disraeli was not English and he was a Jew.
Some people thought he was a bit odd.
He dyed his hair and wore flashy clothes.

The Prime Minister was good with people.
He kept on the right side of Bertie.
He took care not to upset John Brown.
Disraeli and the Queen became close friends.
Victoria gave him many presents.
She sent him flowers from her gardens.
She asked him to stay at Windsor and Balmoral.

Queen Victoria with Mr Disraeli.

Poor Mr Disraeli did not enjoy these visits.
He was always cold
because the Queen left all the windows open.

Disraeli was proud of the British Empire.
The British had taken over land in many countries.
The Prime Minister wanted
the Queen to be seen as a mother figure
in countries in Africa.
In India, Victoria was known as 'the great white queen'.
Disraeli got her the title of Empress of India in 1875.

In 1880 the Liberals won the election.
Mr Gladstone was back in power.
Queen Victoria was sorry to lose Disraeli.
They stayed in touch and wrote to each other.
They had their last meeting at Windsor
in March 1881.

Soon after this Disraeli became ill.
As he lay dying the Queen sent a message.
She asked if she should visit him.
Disraeli's answer was witty as ever.
'Better not', he said. 'She would only ask me
to take a message to Albert.'

9 The Munshi

Queen Victoria grew old.
She was often lonely.
When it was time for her youngest daughter,
Beatrice, to marry, she got upset.
She would not speak to Beatrice.
She wrote notes to her instead.
The young couple had to agree
to come and live with Victoria
after they were married.

In 1887 an Indian Cavalry troop came to London.
The Queen thought the Indian soldiers
looked good in their bright clothes and turbans.
She took two of them on as servants.
One of these was Abdul Karim.
The Queen made up her mind to learn Hindi.
She wanted to know about life in India.
Victoria had no racial prejudice.
She liked people for what they were.

Abdul Karim became her teacher or 'Munshi'.
The Queen became very fond of him.
Soon he took John Brown's place.
He gave orders to the other servants.

Abdul Karim was not as loyal as John Brown.
He began to put on airs and graces.
He wanted his own carriage.
He would not sit with the servants in church.
People even heard him shouting at the Queen.
Then he stole a brooch and sold it.

The Queen took his side.
She would not hear a word against him.
Her ministers were not pleased.
They thought the Munshi might be a spy.
They looked into his background.
He was not a spy but he had stolen and lied.

Then the Munshi wanted
to go on holiday with the Queen
to the South of France.
The Prince of Wales stepped in.
He told the Queen's doctor to speak to her.
He had to tell her it was a bad idea.
The Queen was very angry but she gave in.

10 The End of Her Reign

In 1887 Queen Victoria had her Golden Jubilee.
She had been Queen for 50 years.
She rode through the streets of London.
On her head she wore a lace cap with diamonds.
Medals and coins were made to mark the day.
30,000 children were given Jubilee mugs.
Ten years later, it was her Diamond Jubilee.
Victoria had ruled for 60 years.

Queen Victoria died at Osborne in January 1901.
She was 81 years old.
Her body was taken to London by train.
The streets were hung with white and purple ribbons.
The Queen had said she did not want black.
Her body was pulled through the streets
on a gun carriage.
It was covered with flowers.
Thousands turned out to see her pass by.
The people could not believe the old Queen was dead.

Victoria was laid to rest at Frogmore near Windsor.
Her body was put into the tomb built for Albert
so many years before.
She had gone to join her husband.
They were together at last.

Queen Victoria in old age.